ESCAPE ROUTE

Nick Lyby Skovgaard

ESCAPE ROUTE

- an introduction to Hxaro companies

Hxaro

Escape Route

Cover, illustrations, and
layout by the author
Translated from: 'Flugtvej' by ChatGPT and author

Set in Minion Variable Concept
Publisher: Hxaro, Frederiksberg, Denmark
Print: BoD – Books on Demand, Norderstedt, Germany

ISBN: 978-87-993824-2-2
1st edition

Any surplus from the sale of this publication will be used to promote sustainability. In accordance with the Hxaro principles.

Hxaro Publishing
Nyelandsvej 50
2000 Frederiksberg
Denmark
www.hxaro.dk

To Adrian

In Brief

This is a proposal on how we can address the crises we are currently facing, without being dependent on the world's power holders. The proposal suggests a codex for operating truly sustainable companies, and through them, offers the opportunity to accelerate the necessary transition to sustainability. Utilizing existing structures around business operations makes it easy to get started and impossible for those in power to obstruct. It's a path that distributes power and opportunities for action across the world; out to you and me.

Content:

"If working apart, we are a force powerful enough to destabilise our planet. Surely working together, we are powerful enough to save it."

- David Attenborough

at COP 26 (november 2021)

Dance

30 trillion cells interacting with 39 trillion bacteria in constant physical and chemical exchange, with each other and with everything in their surroundings; together, they constitute me. I do not exist without their constant cooperation, their movements, and communication; the pattern they form for a short while is me. I am embedded in the world, and the world is in me. I am a tiny part of the moment's many carriers of eons of selected mutations, a vanishingly small part of life's dance. This is an infinitely complex interplay that explores and unfolds the possibilities of life. Yet, my dance is poison in the cup from which life drinks.

Introduction

It all started with COP 15 in 2009 in Copenhagen. Of course, in reality, it began much earlier, but it was here that I truly realized that the world's political elite are powerless; the climate crisis will not be addressed through political power alone, as the pressure from industrial and capital interests prevents it. So, I began to look for initiatives that could make a difference, actions that could contribute to reducing our CO2 emissions.

What can I do? What can we do? How can one raise support for larger projects? How to make a real change without it ultimately being dependent on the unattainable grace of the power holders, whether in the form of legislation or investments? All the ideas I could muster always ended up needing either one or the other, or both.

My search led me to read whatever I could find about the climate crisis, and the more I read, the clearer it became that the narrow focus on the climate crisis made the task impossible. The climate crisis is inseparably linked to the biodiversity crisis, to rising inequality, and to the behavior of capitalism on the global stage. Many others reached both insight and solution long before me: The solution is a transition to sustainability; a complete overhaul of the system we live in. In 2015, it became apparent that this insight was globally shared, as all UN member states committed to the 17 Sustainable Development Goals. However, at the start of 2024, progress is lacking; the UN estimates that only 15% of the goals will be achieved with the current pace and course. So, despite recognizing that we have opened the doors to a disaster, we continue into the heat.

We need to change our global system and many of the structures it consists of: the way our economy is interconnected, the way we produce, and the way we consume. Indeed, all the structures associated with our way of doing business.

These structures are difficult to change because they are controlled, supported, and protected by the concentrations of power, as these structures uphold their power. The resistance we encounter when trying to change these structures is extensive and massive, and I don't believe we have time to engage in *that* battle before we accelerate the transition to sustainability. We need to change the entire system and its structures, but for now, we must use the existing structures to initiate change. This is a proposal on how to do it.

"Climate change isn't an 'issue' to add to the list of things to worry about, next to health care and taxes. It is a civilizational wake-up call. A powerful message — spoken in the language of fires, floods, droughts, and extinctions — telling us that we need an entirely new economic model and a new way of sharing this planet. Telling us we need to evolve"

- Naomi Klein

from the book:
'This Changes Everything:
Capitalism vs. the Climate'
(2014)

Chapter 1

When They Dig in the Earth

In 1964, the amount of radioactive fallout, primarily from nuclear weapons testing, reached a global maximum, leaving a distinct geological marker in soil layers across the globe. So, if curious geologists in a distant, distant future were to study the Anthropocene - the age of humans, it would be easy to find. This radioactive marker coincides with the emergence of technofossils; layers of industrially manufactured products that, through a flow-maximizing system, are quickly transformed into waste. Waste that is deposited in the earth, on the ocean floor, frozen into the polar ice, and absorbed into the fabric of life. Moreover, this system changes the chemical composition of the atmosphere and overturns the planet's weather systems. Therefore, it has also been proposed to name the epoch after this system; the Capitalocene - the age of capitalism. The resources for the enormous industrial production are extracted from the earth's reserves, from the world's forests, out of life itself. Earth's reserves are depleted, the forests are burned, and life dies. Capitalism has created a system that destroys the world. Hence, another name has been suggested; the Necrocene - the age of death.

It's up to us to decide if our future geologists will see a brief Capitalocene followed by a long Necrocene period, or if they will see an Anthropocene period containing a flourishing of species, fewer and fewer technofossils, a decrease in the atmospheric content of CO2, and a stabilized sea level in the sediments they excavate eons from now. We stand at the crossroads, you and I, at year zero, a new era starts here, for better or worse. We make the decision for all future generations and for the diverse tapestry of life on the planet. We can continue to leave control to capitalism. Then we can hardly claim to have a geological period named after us, as the Capitalocene will lead the planet directly into the Necrocene.

If we change nothing, we are automatically led down the path cleared and paved by capitalism's insatiable demand for profit.

We can also choose to be the moment in human history where generations and peoples reach out to each other and help each other find a different path, a path that brings our existence into balance with the planet that is our home, a path that ensures the diverse life on Earth. A period where humanity becomes conscious of its power and matures enough to handle it responsibly, a period where humanity protects and nurtures the planet's health, so life in all its wonderful diversity can unfold again. A long Anthropocene period

The Choice:

Continue as now with open eyes: - Necrocene

Not really taking a decision: - Necrocene

The powers holders will handle it: - Necrocene

Conscious collaboration on
the transition to sustainability: -maybe Anthropocene

Maybe... that's the best you'll get.

Chapter 2

Let Go

We feel the wrath of the planet. We understand that there is no more patience in the biosphere's systems. We understand that we are sentencing our children to endure the downfall, and we are assigning future generations to a life in a barren, inhospitable world, where the planet's processes, which have gently supported our development, have become extreme and destructive. Temperatures that boil the water out of life, the sea that will swallow cities, fields, and countries -everywhere. Rain that will drown what the sea hasn't taken. Hurricanes that tear down everything that dares to rise above the ground, crush it, and leave it to the drought and the fire that follows. We do understand it. We just close our eyes. We repress that we are participants in a crime that makes all previous atrocities pale in comparison. We suppress it because we delude ourselves into thinking we have no ability to influence it.

The system we have created has gone haywire, and yet we cling to it. Like army ants, we form one large organism that destroys everything in its path. One organism is driven by the hunt for food, the other by the hunt for profit.

We have to let go of this system, this machine, these monsters that we have invented and bound ourselves to.

"The clock is ticking. We are in the fight of our lives. And we are losing. And our planet is fast approaching tipping points that will make climate chaos irreversible.."

"We are on a highway to climate hell with our foot still on the accelerator."

"Humanity has a choice: cooperate or perish. It is either a Climate Solidarity Pact – or a Collective Suicide Pact."

"Multinational corporations are filling their bank accounts while emptying our world of its natural gifts. Ecosystems have become playthings of profit."

- *António Guterres*
UN Secretary-General
at COP27 (2022)

The System - As We Know It

From the Stone Age to the present, we have invented technologies and systems that ease and improve our existence. Capitalism has accelerated the development of new technologies and ensured their global distribution. As a result, human lives have become longer and materially better. Nevertheless, the negative aspects of capitalism will soon plunge the entire planet into darkness

Companies are the tool we use to make the planet provide us with everything we need. But in a capitalist system, companies are not motivated by selling us what we need; they are motivated by profit. So, they are just as happy to sell us things we do not need. In fact, they just want to sell. Right now, our companies are the most single-minded (legal) entities we can imagine, and we have breathed life into millions of these Golems. We have equipped them with one goal: go out into the world and create as much profit as possible, and then we let them loose. These immortal Golems have grown and done exactly what we asked of them, and they continue to do so. Even now, when it proves to be utterly destructive. They have only one goal and no regard, and the power holders are the Golems' servants, not their helmsmen - they cannot put the genie back in the bottle, in the face of Golems' pursuit of profit, even the power holders are powerless; but to admit that leaves them ... exactly; without power and position in society, so they still pretend they have the ability to curb the madness.

We humans are quite small, and the task is enormous. It seems impossible; we are all just a small part of the machine, small gears that are instantly replaced if we do not deliver the performances required. We are trapped, and it's not only our time and physical existence that are inextricably tied to the machine. We have been conditioned from childhood, so in our adult state, we find it hard to imagine that anything apart from consumption is blissful. Material prosperity that elevates us above our fellow human beings is our success, the size of our success is equal to our distance from others. It is devilishly sarcastic that by adopting the dogma and making it our pursuit of happiness and meaning, we violate everything that actually makes us happy and everything that gives life meaning. We are social beings; we need to be valuable to others. We need to be trustfully together. But when we pursue the ingrained idea of competition and success, we isolate ourselves, seeing each other as resources to be exploited or as competitors to be fought.

Most live in Hades, the very few in Elysium, but instead of the gods' reward for a heroic and righteous life lived, it is our self-created Golem that rewards the owners of capital concentrations with the right to a life in Elysium's eternal spring, with rivers of wine. In Hades' gloomy, dark passages, everyone else run around, deprived of their time, while under Golem's manipulations, they dig, burn, press, and scrape the earth empty of life. For Golem's task is to make the rich richer. Not to bring us all to Elysium.

The activities of global corporations shift in pursuit of the cheapest labor and the least regulations. In doing so, they erode workers' rights and increase the gap between the rich and the poor. The rich get richer, and capital concentrations grow larger. Inequality rises, and meanwhile, we all try to stay afloat economically. Unfortunately, by doing so, we merely support and maintain the system that drains the joy and life out of us, while steering us all directly into the Necrocene.

Power concentrates, and the political system, under the constant increasing pressure of capital, ends up as its extended arm. The road away from disasters is not built by capitalism; there is no sustainability at the end of this system, no meaningful work life, no meaningful life, no life.

In Hades, we survive, we try to adapt, and when we are about to be choked by *homo economicus*' too tight tie, we believe it's our own fault. We are taken hostage and live at the mercy of the system, and the power we are subjected to is so violent that, to avoid having our psyche torn apart, we throw our own goals and dreams on the pyre and make Golem's goals our own; a worldwide Stockholm Syndrome. We are capitalism's obedient servants, we are consumers, we are the great burden on the planet's climate and biodiversity, we are maintainers of a system that increases the world's inequality, we are dissolvers of life's fabric. But we are not completely blind to the damage we do, we just can't find the way out. So we continue to burn the earth, kill life, and pursue a mad goal.

When we go to work, we cannot decide whether to do harmful or sustainable things. That decision is made by the demand for profit. We are only useful servants as long as we enable our Golem to please its owners. However, most owners are shareholders who merely speculate in securities; they have no real interest in the companies themselves, only in their ability to generate profit and growth. Thus, there's no one to introduce reason into corporate decisions, no desire to focus a bit less on profit and a bit more on stopping the destruction we cause. Profit is the only demand of the owners, and the only goal of the Golems. Another twist in our self-preserving and world-destroying system is that we are owners ourselves. Through our pension funds, we too own the companies and make the same demands for profit. We, the workers of the Western world. Most workers in the Global South have no or insufficient pension; they are life-long bound to the wheel, forced to serve the capital concentrations' demands for more and more profit. Until they no longer have any market value and are expelled by the profit mechanism.

At the very top sit the concentrations of capital, like heads on a Hydra, uncoordinated, striving for nothing but profit. They are systemic concentrations of power, not individuals; their will is merely manifested through people. Their unstoppable pursuit is defined by capitalism's demand for profit, with humans as tools. Each head impacts the world with the aim of maximizing their own capital growth, and the collective power of the Hydra is immense

There is a great focus on the fortunes of the wealthiest individuals, but these are atypical concentrations of capital because the single owner can actually choose how the economic power is used. The rest are bound by the profit goal; hedge funds, commodity funds, pension funds, venture capital funds, multinational corporations, technology giants, pharmaceutical conglomerates, family dynasties, fortunes controlled by autocratic states, and criminal wealth. They have different tools to make countries, governments, populations, and individuals comply with their wishes. Depending on the type, methods range from advertising, influence campaigns, lobbying, through support to political campaigns, research funding, placement of workplaces, to blackmail, threats, and murder. What they have in common is not the methods; it is the demand for profit and the demand for growth. It is the capital concentrations that hold the power. Not individuals, not populations, not governments, and the power of capital concentrations just grows and grows.

It's pointless to get angry over their actions, even though they are clearly destroying the world. Neither anger nor prayers will make them change their behavior; there is no attack that could threaten or shake them, and no prayer move them. They control the system and will continue to demand profit from the world's companies, and the companies will continue to deliver by exploiting the earth, life, and people until there is nothing left to exploit. And we will continue to work for the companies and consume their products. How else are we to live? We are well aware that the world looks like this, but if there's nothing we can do to change it, we resign or become ill. We can't change the system through the current democratic processes; the power does not lie with the elected officials. Revolutions throw everything to the ground, and when it's picked up, it turns out to work worse than before, and power is still in the hands of a few, albeit different, hands. Personal choices and rejections, to influence the market and make companies produce sustainably, are a very long process, constantly opposed by the companies' need to squeeze a little more profit out of the products they have already developed, and it places an unbearable pressure on the individual. We need an emergency exit. We must work in the smoke-filled corridors of this system while we build an emergency exit away from here. An entrance to something new.

power and motive

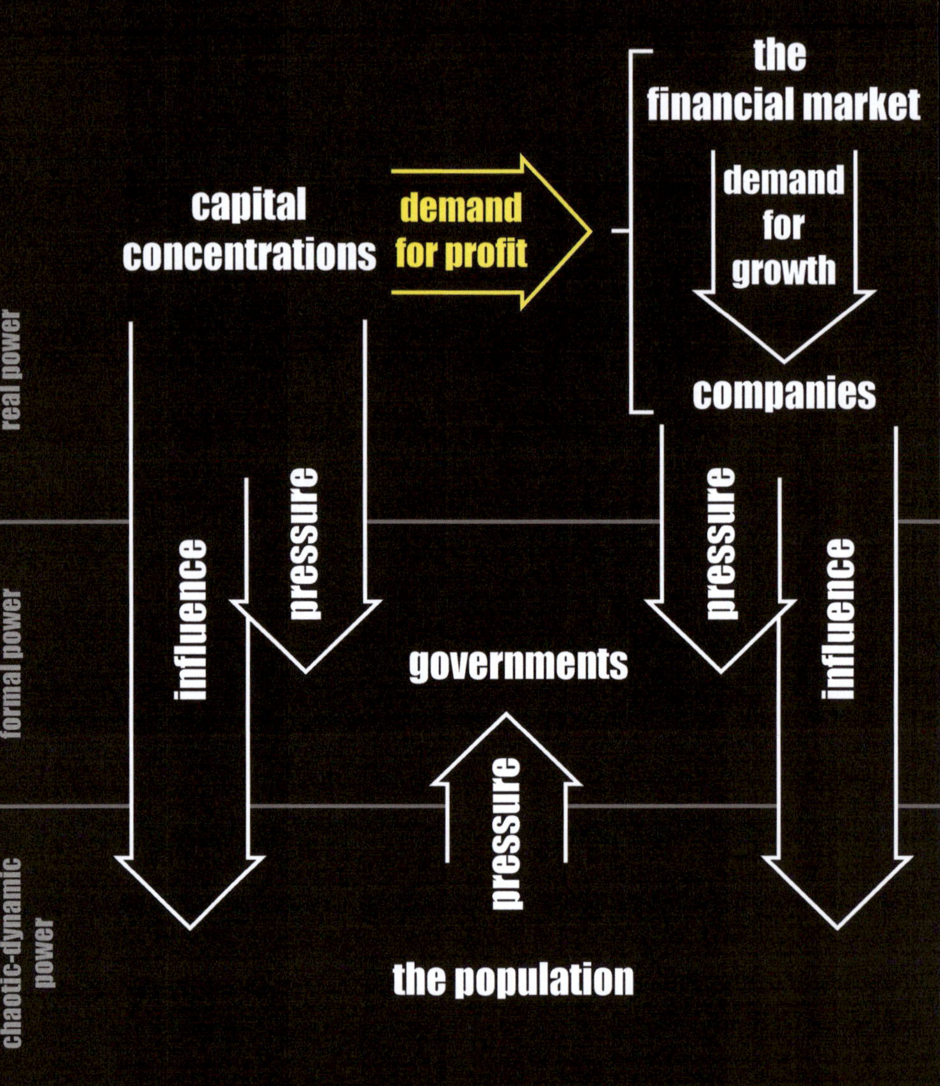

life - the sea - the earth - the atmosphere

The illustration shows four spheres: The Real Power, The Formal Power, The Chaotic-Dynamic Power, and The Powerless. The areas are occupied by various actors, and the arrows illustrate the demands, pressures, and influences that exist between them.

The Real Power:
Capital concentrations, the financial market, and companies together control The Real Power; to such an extent that today they *are* The Real Power. Their significant power is used to pressure and influence world governments and populations in the direction that best serves the demand for profit. It is not a coordinated effort; it is just a natural consequence of needing to generate as much profit as possible.
Among the three, companies occupy a special place; they are the ones who directly affect the world, they are the ones who use the earth's resources, and they are the ones who create all the necessities we need.

The Formal Power:
The governments and political systems that manage the areas in which the companies operate. They are in ongoing negotiation with The Real Power about the level of freedom companies can achieve. A negotiation that can have a very different character depending on the country's form of governance, rule of law, and the amount of corruption. The actors in The Formal Power can make demands on local companies but are powerless against multinational corporations that let their activities flow to where the demands are weakest and the profit is greatest.

The Chaotic-Dynamic Power:
People, all of us, the world's population, the populations of the world. Divided into groups defined by affiliations and beliefs, in conflict with each other. A chaotic power that does not focus its energy but uses it in internal struggles. But also a dynamic and potentially very large power if it manages to move collectively.

The Powerless:
The planet that provides all the resources, the commons that are depleted, everything we should protect and nurture so it can support life for our descendants. The truly powerless; all that we destroy, all that has no voice; life itself, the fabric of life. The seemingly weakest and most yielding, which will still remove us from the equation and start over if we continue as we do now.

"They [the ruling classes] know it, and they would like to address the climate crisis: 'It fails for structural reasons - because the very core of our capitalist system opposes the necessary steps in the transition.'"

- Jason Hickel

Author of the book: 'Less is more'
Quote from: Dagbladet Information (10 december 2022)
(my translation)

Chapter 3

The Emergency Exit

Humanity has lost the reins, and the capitalist system has run amok, spurred on by the dictum that creates all the entangled unhealthy patterns that constantly increase inequality, steal people's time, bodies, and thoughts, destroy the planet's fabric of life, and are grafted into our perception of reality and into millions of immortal Golems as their sole goal; the demand for profit.

Everywhere in the world, there have been values that Capital needed to convert into profit, and the tool for this task is companies. The structures surrounding business operations are widespread throughout the world, they are quite uniform, and geared so that trade can take place across the globe. This is because it serves the interest of the profit goal. Capital has used its cocktail of pressure and promises to standardize the opportunity to conduct business. Regardless of continent, country, culture, norms, language, and political system, private companies are guaranteed their freedom to operate. So perhaps we can use companies to redirect the rivers of money and power flowing to Capital's Elysium, and instead let them become streams, rivers, and brooks that fertilize the soil of transition. Companies are the system's agents of change, and by using them, *we* get the opportunity to transform the world.

At first it may seem strange to use companies to create balance in our relationship with the world when it is precisely the operations of companies that enslave us and wring all value out of life and the earth. But that's only because companies do exactly what we have asked them to; they pursue the goal. The extermination of life on earth is just an unfortunate side effect. All companies driven by the demand for profit will extract more resources from the world than they give back, leaving the earth barren and buried in discarded, rejected, and broken people and waste. But companies produce our necessities of life, and companies produce a multitude of products and services that we want. We need the companies, we shop with them, and we will keep shopping with them, out of necessity and out of desire.

So what happens if we create companies whose goal is sustainability; - not profit... is that even possible?

The initial reaction is no, it cannot be done. Who would start and run a business if there's no chance of making a profit; the reward for risking house and home, the reward for working day and night, compensation for never seeing one's children, the proof of success, the opportunity to rise above others? Who would invest in companies that do not deliver a return, that do not offer endless growth? How could a company compete if it takes social responsibility, pays its employees fairly, if it does not partake in the plunder of nature's resources, and if it gives back to the world at least as much as it takes from it?

But it *may* be possible, it's the same maybe that makes the Anthropocene a possibility. Some choose to shed the *homo economicus* costume and begin the journey towards sustainability, as recognition and as a way of working. It's already happening. What I propose is a declaration, some common guidelines, that enable us to support and strengthen each other, a way to increase our chances of surviving in a world of profit-focused companies. If we succeed in creating truly sustainable compagnies, then we have a tool that can change structures in the system and ultimately the system itself. A tool that can initiate and spread sustainable solutions across the globe, and if we do it right, it may happen very, very quickly.

Hxaro

In the Kalahari Desert of southern Africa, the San people have developed a trust-based system that ensures their survival. The San people live in small groups scattered across the desert, and when natural disasters force a group from their home, they move in with a neighboring group until it is possible to return home. The mutual trust is maintained in times without disasters through the exchange of small gifts; a song, a dance, a piece of handicraft, and they have done this for generations upon generations, and perhaps the system's origin goes all the way back to the San people's earliest ancestors who inhabited the area 70,000 years ago. This trust-based system is called Hxaro.

We are raised in a system that fosters mistrust, but to create a sustainable future, we need trust. Building fundamental trust is a long process, but we do not need to start with a complete and blind trust; we can manage with less while we build a system with a strength like that of the San people. We need to help each other; we are one large group exposed to disasters we ourselves have invoked, and the only place we can flee to is into a sustainable future, *that* is the only safe place.

The San people's Hxaro is based on a mutual promise to help each other and continuous confirmation of that promise. We need companies that make a promise to work to create a sustainable world, and we need them to continuously confirm that they are serious about it. I call them Hxaro companies.

"We can no longer let people in power decide what hope is. Hope is not passive. Hope is not 'blah blah blah.' Hope is telling the truth. Hope is taking action. And hope always comes from the people."

- Gretha Thunberg

at Youth4Climate PreCOP26 (2021)

The Commitment

Hxaro companies declare that they strive for sustainability and adhere to three principles:

-They co-create
-They are transparent
-Their surplus goes to sustainability

These three principles collectively form an alternative to the demand for profit. The principles support each other and form a circle. The circle of the three principles makes everything visible, illuminates the path to sustainability, creates connections between people, and distributes power to all who wish to create a sustainable future.

Co-creation is necessary to access as much knowledge as possible and to ensure that the products created are in fact used and actually replace unsustainable solutions. Co-creation reaches out to everyone who knows something about a topic, everyone who has ideas on how to solve a problem or replace a need, and to everyone who just wants to be involved; it's a democratization of the development of products. It's a conversation that crosses nationalities, generations, professions, and all other divides. It's an engaging factor, and open co-creation promotes trust.

Transparency guarantees the sincere desire to strive for sustainability, partly by making salaries, accounts, business partners, development, materials, and business models visible to all, but also by making all ideas freely available and allowing copying. Transparency builds trust that the company's declaration of striving for sustainability is serious.

The surplus of a Hxaro company goes to sustainability, so when a surplus is made, it is used to promote sustainability through the development of new solutions, donations, or loans to start new Hxaro companies, or support for organizations working towards sustainability. Anything that meaningfully spreads sustainable solutions and promotes the transition to sustainability. And sustainability creates equality, which in turn increases trust.

The pursuit of sustainability that Hxaro companies declare they will follow does not mean they commit to being sustainable from day one in all aspects, only that they will create more sustainable solutions than the (at any time) existing solutions. They commit to acting sustainably internally as well as externally, and to constantly strive to do better and better in collaboration with their users, with other Hxaro companies, and with the society around them. There is no Hxaro certificate, there are no fixed rules or procedures, there is only the company's declaration to follow the principles. This means that each company can work in the way they find most meaningful in their context, and the evaluation of whether it is a beneficial path is made by their network, by all those who help the company with development and operations, and everyone who trades with them.

Aside from their radically different goal, Hxaro companies operate in the world like any other businesses. They are subject to the same laws, pay taxes, have salaried employees, and they compete with traditional companies for market share. One might think that this places Hxaro companies at a disadvantage, but when they enter the competition, they change the rules. They bring more to the transaction than just a focus on the lowest price. With their practice of directing profits towards sustainability, utilizing their services becomes an investment in the future, a contribution to entering a tolerable Anthropocene. In many cases, their products will likely be priced similarly to those of traditional companies because they can use their extra leeway; the portion of earnings that would otherwise be paid out as profit, for any additional costs of the sustainable solution.

So, when we use companies to spread sustainable solutions, we are engaging with a central structure, for this is where all the activity in the world economy is, where all services, products, and necessities of life are created, and where all decisions about how this is done are made. This is where the human world is shaped and driven. And for every traditional company that is replaced by a Hxaro company, the effect is doubled; an exploiter is replaced by a builder.

Anyone can start a company, making it a field that you and I can play on, and when we start a Hxaro company and begin our operations in the market, we divert money flows away from accumulation by capital concentrations, and back towards the work of transitioning to sustainability. This characteristic makes the development self-reinforcing, and the transition can suddenly gain momentum. There is nothing in Hxaro companies that requires the grace of the power holders. Hxaro companies follow the system's rules and use its structures but are not governed by the system's destructive creed.

power and another motive

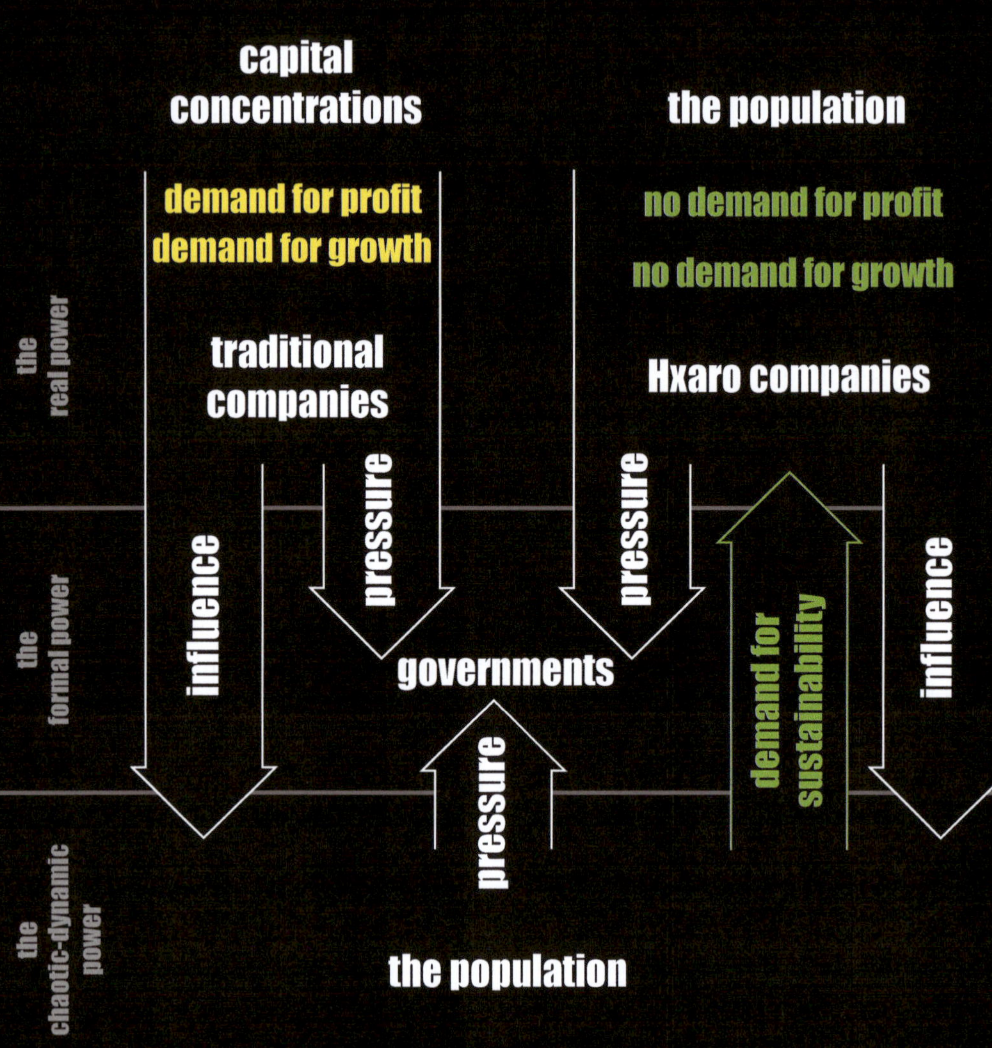

the powerless

life - the sea - the earth - the atmosphere

The illustration has the same structure as the illustration: POWER AND MOTIVE, but here the proposed Hxaro companies and the demands, pressures, and influences they will bring are inserted.

On the left side is the current power dynamics: capital concentrations demanding profit from traditional companies. On the right side, we find the Hxaro companies, which operate side by side with traditional companies and thus come to occupy a place in the realm of real power. The motivation of Hxaro companies is to satisfy the demand for sustainability, and this demand comes from the world's population, which lifts the population, or rather; lifts the population's specific wish for a transition to sustainability into the sphere of real power.

Hxaro companies will pressure governments to facilitate the transition and will influence populations through the opportunities they create and the debate they raise. Examples of the possible transition will also give the populations' pressure on their political systems greater strength.

The top three spheres are the domain of humanity, where we decide how our relationship with everything our existence rests upon should be: do we continue to hollow out the planet until it can no longer bear our weight, do we continue to suffocate life until the entire fabric dissolves, do we continue to play with matches, or do we take care of that witch has no voice, the powerless, the bottom but first sphere.

So, when we run genuinely sustainable businesses; Hxaro companies, we not only create sustainable alternatives to existing products - though we do that too - but we also open the door to a whole world of new products and services that aren't profitable in the traditional sense and therefore don't exist today. Hxaro companies pave the way for ways of contributing and collaborating that are unthinkable in traditional businesses. Helping traditional companies without receiving anything in return is akin to giving your money away to the company's owners; it's senseless. Helping Hxaro companies without getting anything in return is to work for the transition. It's meaningful, and every contribution brings us closer to a sustainable world. Hxaro companies invite everyone in, thereby gaining access to an inexhaustible reservoir of knowledge and assistance that traditional companies can't access even through payment. The collaboration strengthens our trust in each other and increases our chances of finding solutions to the challenges we face, it enhances our resilience, and no matter what world awaits us, our chances are better if we have practiced working together.

Here and now, we must be able to devote our time to something meaningful. All Hxaro companies share the goal of sustainability, and they help each other to achieve it - and we help them. Suddenly, a Hxaro company offering to repair clothes, furniture, and technology can actually make a mark on the market. Not because it 'pays off' within a narrow profit logic, but because it pays off from a sustainability perspective; - it's meaningful, and because it's meaningful, the company enjoys support in many different ways; volunteer help, both practical and in the form of knowledge and expertise, donations that support operations; e.g., premises for repair and storage, and donations of objects, materials, and tools. In addition, there is a willingness to support by doing business with the company.

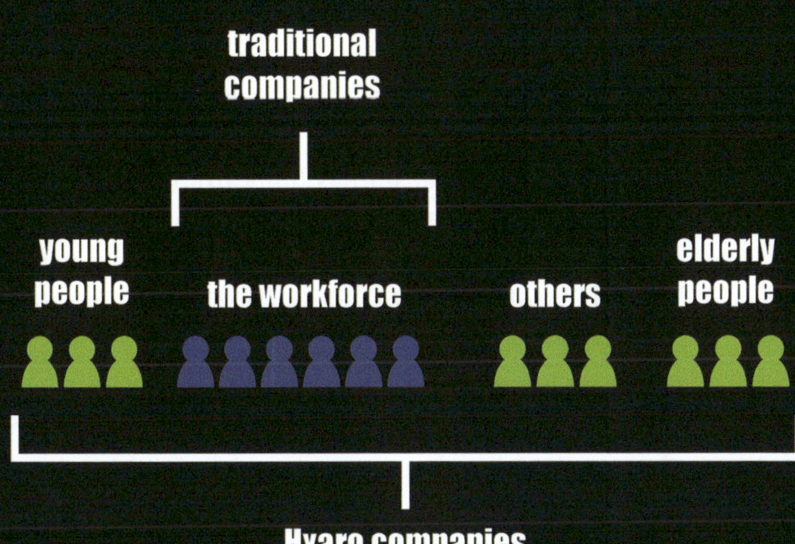

When Hxaro-companies develop and operate sustainable solutions, they can draw on practical help, innovative power, and experience from all of us, regardless of life situation and age.

We participate because it makes sense to transition the world to sustainability, and because it's an opportunity to act on the crises.

Our chance to build and provide hope.

The ’we’ that helps is very broadly composed; we need each other and all the knowledge and experience we collectively possess. There’s a real need for all our efforts, energy, creativity, and willingness to act - we genuinely need everyone. All generations have something to contribute, all groups have something to offer, you and I have something to bring to the table.

We utilize the structure capitalism has built around businesses, not the logic businesses operate with. We don’t protect our ideas; we share them. Any solution that contributes to the transition should be spread as quickly as possible, so our song, our dance, our handicraft are the solutions we create and release so everyone can use them, so everyone can adapt them to their reality, and everyone can further develop them. And when they flow back to us, they’ve become stronger, larger, and have inspired even more flourishing ideas.

When Hxaro companies don’t protect rights and aren’t motivated by the size of ’their own’ profit, it becomes possible to copy, combine, and fearlessly interweave Hxaro companies with each other. They all share the same goal, so they don’t need to think about maximizing the benefits from a collaboration individually. They need to think about how we all can achieve the most sustainability, and how the transition can happen fastest.

Chapter 4

Locally

Our production chains span the globe, allowing production to take place where labor is cheapest, environmental regulations are weakest, and raw materials are least expensive. This means that goods and materials are transported back and forth across the world, and this energy-demanding transport is powered by fossil fuels. The climate footprint of 'globally' manufactured goods is significantly larger than the footprint of locally produced goods. In short; in many, many cases, the local solutions will be the most sustainable. This also means that most of our Hxaro companies will be built on local communities, where we meet face to face. Where it's possible to walk in from the street and participate in the work for sustainability, where the barrier to becoming part of the transition is almost non-existent. Local communities that have room for and need all generations; communities that are the companies' supporters, developers, ambassadors, and customers.

Even though we develop collaboratively, the responsibility lies with the owner(s) of the company. So, Hxaro companies are not necessarily collectively or democratically led, and decisions can be made without consensus in the company. But if trust in the management disappears, the company will not survive. The same applies if a management awards itself an unreasonably high salary. The assessment of the fairness in salaries is made by the network around the company, not as a formalized process, but if the perception is that the resources are managed unreasonably, it will be addressed, and if that doesn't work, trade and support will drop, and eventually, the employees will leave the company, and possibly start a clone of it, which will pay at a level perceived as reasonable. This also implies that some will be extraordinarily rewarded for their effort, and that *this* will be perceived as reasonable. But since salaries are also part of transparency, it's hard to imagine the exorbitant salaries we see today. There's no problem with those who put in the work being rewarded; the problem is that capitalism distributes enormous rewards, without the recipients contributing anything, while others work for a wage so low they can barely survive.

Chapter 5

Oases

Every Hxaro company is a spore that falls on fertile ground in the capitalist desert. When it sprouts, a whole small community arises around it, a local blooming that sends new spores out into the world, solutions that can be made to grow in new fertile places. At the same time, the soil around the Hxaro company is nurtured so other initiatives can emerge. People of all ages, bringing thousands of valuable spores and seeds in the form of knowledge and ideas, will gravitate towards the oases that appear in the desert. Oases with springs that grow the more we draw from them. Oases that let their green leaves cast protective shadows from the merciless sun of profit. Oases that restore a fertile layer of soil in the pulverized world left by capitalism.

It starts with the world's privileged, with us, because we have the time and the means. We need to initiate the transition, and Hxaro companies will assist us in this. We invest the time and surplus we've been granted as a birthright due to our random placement in the world's hierarchy, and we use this gift to make it possible to create sustainable solutions worldwide, even in places where the standard of living needs to rise, even where there is no one with time or surplus resources. Places where Hxaro companies will only exist if they offer actual paid jobs. So, we and our companies make ideas, knowledge, and resources available to everyone who wants the transition. We don't show up with ready-made solutions; we create solutions for our own local reality, and if they can be used, even just half of them, then do so, use what makes sense, discard the rest, adapt to your local reality and pass it on. The power to create change is distributed out into the world, in this way we expand the 'we' that gains access to power. Power goes out to local collaborations, which each, with their knowledge of local conditions combined with the knowledge, experience, and resources we globally possess, initiate the transition.

The networks around Hxaro companies share and distribute ideas and knowledge free to use, and by doing so, we give each other the power to create change, bypassing the power holders.

The protection of ideas is made so publicly disclosed ideas cannot be patented. By developing solutions publicly, we don't prevent important and effective ideas from falling into the hands of traditional companies, but we ensure that their use and dissemination are not slowed down. The ideas developed in traditional companies are usually protected by patents that last 20 years, and during that period, the company controls where solutions are available and their cost. We can't wait 20 years for sustainable solutions to become available everywhere; we need to use and improve them now. The world needs them spread everywhere as quickly as possible.

The openness is a way to create new commons from which we all can harvest ideas, and since we can all move around here and plant, nurture, and harvest ideas, while constantly talking to each other and helping each other, we can move from idea to product and business in a very short time. We are not hindered by having to keep anything secret; we can talk to everyone, not just those we pay, and we can even expect to get help from the most knowledgeable in all fields whether they are retired or work in a traditional company. It is a concrete and meaningful way to work for the transition, and everyone gets the possibility to contribute what they can. It's a way to make the world more bearable for us now, and for our children and grandchildren in the future, it's a way to find and give hope.

Most people want to contribute to the transition, but not to be taken for fools; we need to see that others are contributing too. We don't want to be met with wagging fingers and moralizing, but we would like to participate in a collective endeavor. We are in a collective action dilemma. No one does anything until everyone does something and everyone is waiting. But Hxaro companies are doing something, and they are visible and engaging, close by and hopefully soon everywhere. They go trustingly first and open a possible path to the transition, suddenly everyone can join in.

The illustration shows how ideas and knowledge, which arise or become available to traditional companies (illustrated with squares), are presented to capital concentrations in an attempt to secure financing for commercialization, and how knowledge is isolated from other companies and the public. In this way, not only capital is concentrated but also knowledge, and only ideas with profit potential are promoted. Ideas that threaten existing business models will be suppressed or delayed if possible. (Given the power that capital concentrations wield, this is probably often possible). The chosen ideas are protected by IP rights and patents, meaning their dissemination for general use is delayed for about 20 years.

Next to this, we have Hxaro companies (illustrated with stars), which share and develop ideas and knowledge in interaction with the public, and do not seek exclusive rights to ideas; if an idea promotes sustainability, it should not be delayed but implemented as broadly and as quickly as possible.

access to knowledge and ideas

traditional companies

knowledge and ideas are isolated and protected

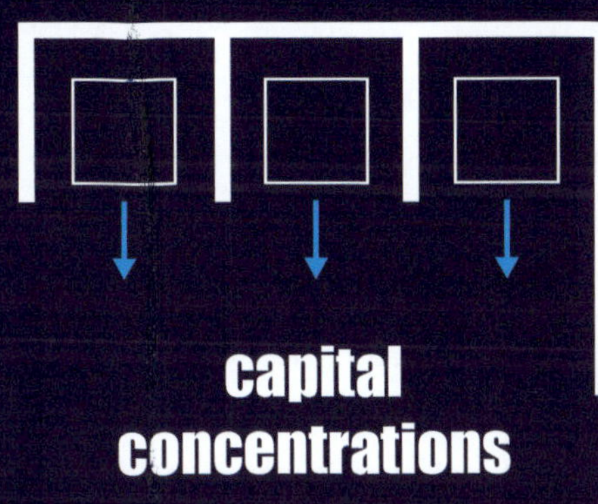

capital concentrations

ideas that generate profit are promoted

Hxaro companies

knowledge and ideas are shared

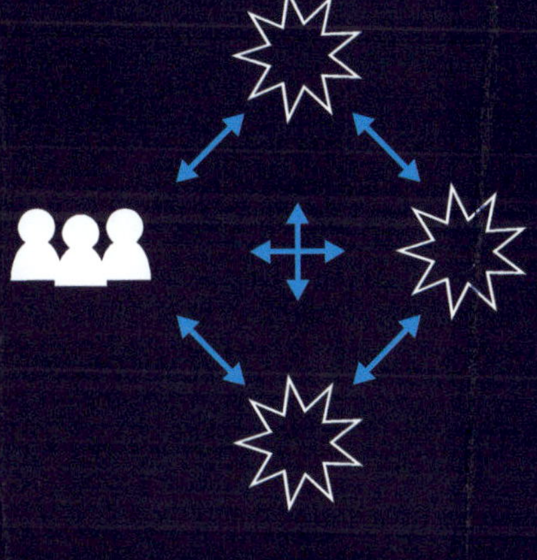

ideas that deliver sustainability are promoted

Where do you want to spend your time, your work, and your money?

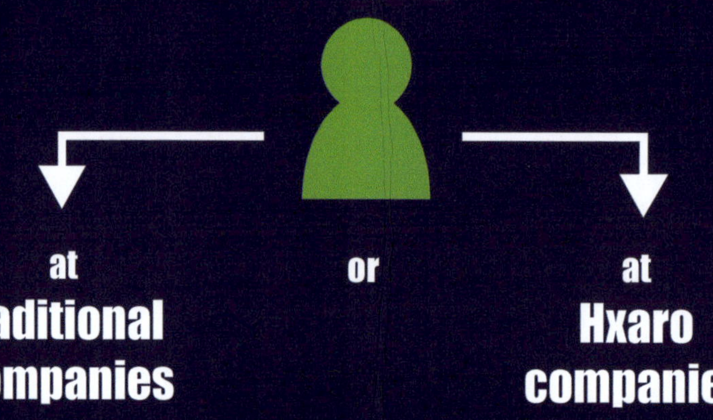

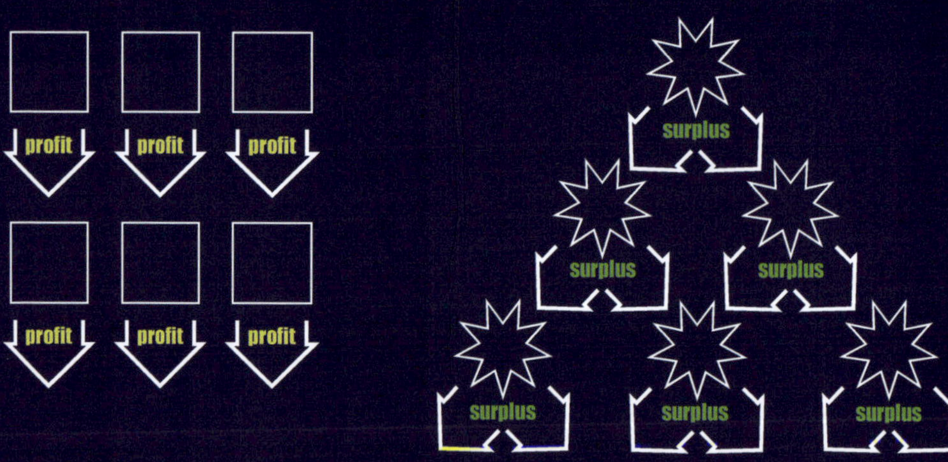

capital concentrations

transition to sustainability

Chapter 6

Off the road and onto the trails

It might not be as difficult to break free from capitalism as we imagine; perhaps it just requires having a choice.

Imagine two completely identical companies, with employees in all roles; production, sales, service, management. Maybe it's the company you work for now. You receive the same salary, the same conditions, work with the same things as now. One is traditionally driven, so profits go to the owners. The other is a Hxaro company, so the surplus goes to sustainability. Which one would you prefer to work for, which one would you prefer to shop from? Although, of course, it's unlikely that a Hxaro company would be a 1:1 copy of a traditional company. The Hxaro company wouldn't just pass on surplus to promote sustainability; it would itself be a more sustainable way to tackle the task. When Hxaro companies are a reality, it's no longer impossible to live and work in a way that promotes the transition. And if we return to the question of who wants to start companies without the possibility of getting part of the profits forever, maybe we shouldn't look at the traditional entrepreneurs but more at ourselves. When it's possible to test ideas without a huge risk, and with a degree of help and support so you don't have to work day and night or risk house and home, and when success isn't measured by how high you rise above others but by how closely we can work together, then maybe many of us will.

Yet, no Hxaro companies will arise without money to start them, and since they don't offer returns to investors, traditional venture capital isn't accessible. So, start-up funds must be found in other ways. To start the first Hxaro companies, broad support is needed, crowdfunding, pre-purchases, loans, donations, foundation support, and volunteer work. Later, the surplus from ongoing Hxaro companies will likely become the main source of start-up capital for new initiatives.

Stepping off the road onto the trails is not an immediate transition to sustainable living... how could it be? It's choosing to move activities from the old to the new system, and voluntarily engaging in expanding the new. The presence of an alternative, the very possibility of *working* for the transition, can provide hope. Not everyone needs to embrace the idea and switch to sustainability. We plant the ideas, open the opportunities, and offer alternatives, and when there are enough alternatives, they might end up becoming the norm.

"Sociologist Damon Centola estimates that the critical tipping point for changing everyone's behavior is a committed minority of 25%."

from the Climate Book by Gretha Thunberg (2023)

Chapter 7

Consensus on one single matter

In the 2000s, we believed that the Internet would lead to a new Enlightenment, that global access to knowledge would automatically lead to an increased common understanding of the world, and that the ability to converse with everyone everywhere would boost our trust in each other so we could find common solutions to the world's problems. It didn't turn out that way. However, with Hxaro companies, we might be able to reopen that ambition, albeit on a smaller scale. We can limit our common understanding of the world to an agreement on the importance of transitioning to sustainability, and through conversation, reverse the order, so we find solutions together and thereby build trust in each other.

The crucial agreement on the transition is already a reality. Not only in the form of unanimous support for the UN's 17 Sustainable Development Goals but also among populations worldwide, climate and biodiversity crises are among the greatest concerns. So, on this *one* point, we have a common interest, and with Hxaro companies as a tool, we can act on our concerns, without agreement on anything else.

Hxaro companies naturally start messy and uncoordinated, and the only ones who can judge whether a company is doing something sensible are the local supporters around the company. Gradually, however, platforms will emerge that gather and organize the data and ideas generated around, forums will be created where solutions are discussed, copied, and developed, and tools made to calculate how sustainable an idea is. There will be crowdfunding and crowdlending sites where ideas are pitched and seek support, and tools to assist with the establishment and operation of the companies.

Over the last 20 years, a range of technologies and tools have been created that give us possibilities that have never existed before. A whole palette that we can use, borrow from, or further develop; collaboration platforms, open source, crowdfunding, social media, blockchain, video meetings, online education, digital production technologies, and most recently AI. Only now is the opportunity for as broad, both geographically and interpersonally, collaboration as Hxaro companies require present, and perhaps together we can bring it all into play for the benefit of the transition.

Every single Hxaro company is a very small ice cube in a very large and warm ocean. It's not each company individually that makes a difference, but the mountains of ice they can become when they grow from each other's crystals, allowing the collective mass to cool the planet, and just before that; perhaps also the brains of politicians. Today, innovation comes solely from companies and only in forms that increase earnings. But when genuinely sustainable companies lead the way and show what possibilities there are, politicians who actually want the transition have far better cards at hand in their work to enact legislation that promotes sustainability. Once we get there, our chances significantly increase, -and wouldn't it be nice if we could start talking about what kind of society we want to create and what the good life is, instead of talking about how we maintain the society we have, in a world falling apart around us.

Capitalism constantly generates heightened needs in order to sell new and more products. Capitalism needs you to feel a void, or at least to perceive that something is missing. You are fundamentally meant to be dissatisfied and seek fulfillment through consumption. This is meaningless. A sustainable society is interested in you lacking nothing, in you enjoying life, being satisfied, not needing to seek fulfillment through consumption. The sustainable abundance is a fundamental equality that guarantees everyone access to the most basic necessities of life and the opportunity to live as they wish. The sustainable society aims for an abundance of what makes us happy and allows us to thrive; cooperation, trust, recognition, and the opportunity to pursue the paths that fascinate us.

So we're not giving up much when we engage in the transition, instead we maybe filling our lives with meaning. Perhaps capitalism is deprivation disguised as abundance, and sustainability is abundance without disguise.

The Conclusion - The Hope - The Beginning

An era has reached its end, the world is falling apart, and it feels as though time itself is broken. We feel it clearly, and we have a growing desire to stop the destruction and repair what can still be saved. This creates a pressure looking for a way out. Hxaro companies can help make a hole in the dike, and when that happens, the flow will make the hole bigger and bigger, allowing our actions and ideas to flood and reclaim the commons that capitalism has taken over, exploited, and is now suffocating completely. The more that flows through, the larger areas will be fertilized, and hopefully, life will once again have a chance.

Here and now, Hxaro companies can be a tool to accelerate the transition to sustainability, but over time, their actions can contribute to a fairer world where power is not concentrated in the hands of a few but is instead distributed so that more and more share in it.

Perhaps we harbor an unrealized potential that we can release through the transition. Perhaps we can let our small part of the dance nourish life's infinitely complicated flower. Perhaps we can become the most beautiful version of ourselves when we choose to lay the foundations for a sustainable Anthropocene, when we choose to transcend our own limited time and existence, when we choose life.

"In my lifetime, I've witnessed a terrible decline. In yours, you could and should witness a wonderful recovery."

- David Attenborough

at COP 26 (november 2021)

Afterword

This text is addressed to all of you who, like me, are searching for a possible way out of the disaster we find ourselves in; this is the Escape Route, Hxaro companies are the Emergency Exit.

It is a proposal for everyone who wants to act on the disasters, everyone who feels that the political system and those in power in general have failed. For all who feel the urgency, but lack the opportunity. It is a way around the power holders, a way to build hope.

It's not easy ...yet; there are no Hxaro companies we can assist or do business with, nor any tools that ease the process when we want to create truly sustainable businesses. We don't even have a network yet, so let's start by finding each other and then tread the new trails together.

Write to me at nick@hxaro.dk if you want to join the effort, or take the ideas you can use with you on your own journey towards sustainability.

In hope of a kinder future

Nick Lyby Skovgaard

Appendix

The previous sections aimed to describe how Hxaro companies operate. What follows here is an attempt to identify some projects that could make it easier for Hxaro companies to get started. These projects are themselves Hxaro companies and can be challenged and replaced if they do not deliver credibly, or if they start to act like concentrations of power.

I believe a platform where we can share thoughts and projects, where we can help and support each other, is crucial. A kind of fusion between a social network and a crowdfunding platform, possibly supported by an AI language model, which helps to sort and identify relevant information and contacts for the project we are working on and makes it possible to find knowledge no matter where it comes from and in what language it is presented. Available on the platform could also be a range of tools/services for Hxaro companies; legal assistance, help with setting up a company, assessment of ideas' contributions to a sustainable world, accounting and auditing assistance, etc. Some of these may be global in nature, others local.

One approach to finding ideas for Hxaro companies could be to look at the world locally and try to identify waste, overconsumption, injustice, and recklessness towards nature, and from there formulate an alternative that can satisfy the needs and solve the tasks that truly exist, but in a sustainable way. The world is a closed system, and sometimes (not always) it helps to consider an area, a city, or a country as a closed system when thinking about solutions; nothing in, nothing out, we have what we have, so how do we use it best.

Good luck with your work!

"Your actions matter. No action or voice is too small to make a difference."

-Vanessa Nakate

at COP 26 (november 2021)